I want to say a massive thank you to my four children for continually inspiring me and for pushing me towards my greatness - you have always been my biggest cheerleaders.

Because of the four of you, I am me.

May God continue to cover you, leading you towards your greatness, guiding your footsteps to walk into an abundantly blessed life.

T, K, A, T

Mummy love's you forever!

Early in the morning, Taye lays sleeping in his bed; he felt a *tingling* feeling happening to his head.

Taye **jumped** out of his sleep to see what was going on. For some **crazy** reason his *hair* started to get **long!**

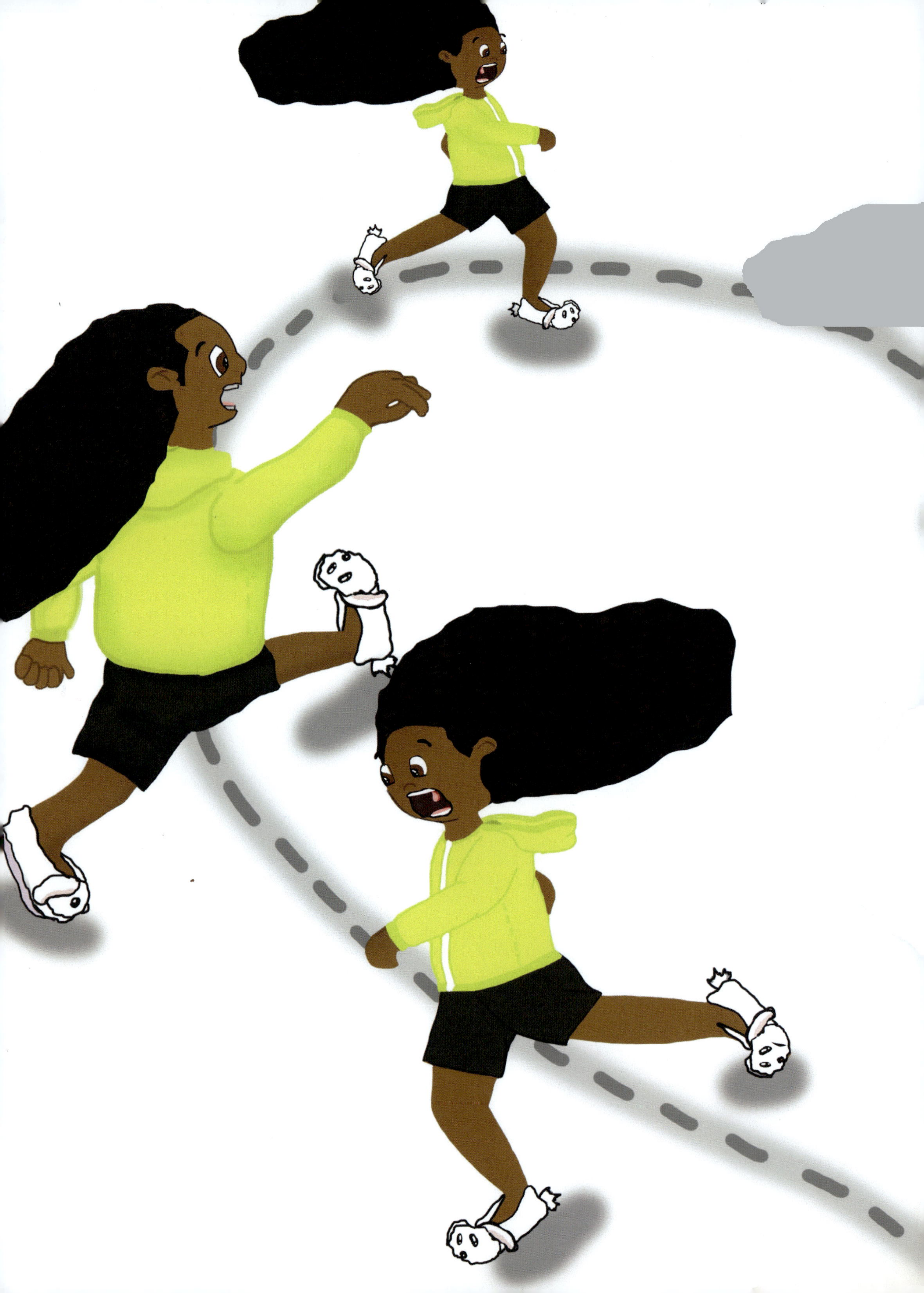

Taye's *hair* started to **grow** and **grow**, getting **longer** and **thicker** by the minute...

And with it growing longer

no one knew what to do with it!

Taye's *hair* continued to **grow** and **grow** longer than anything ever seen before. It grew **SUPER**, duper, curly, long

"I think it can touch the moon!"

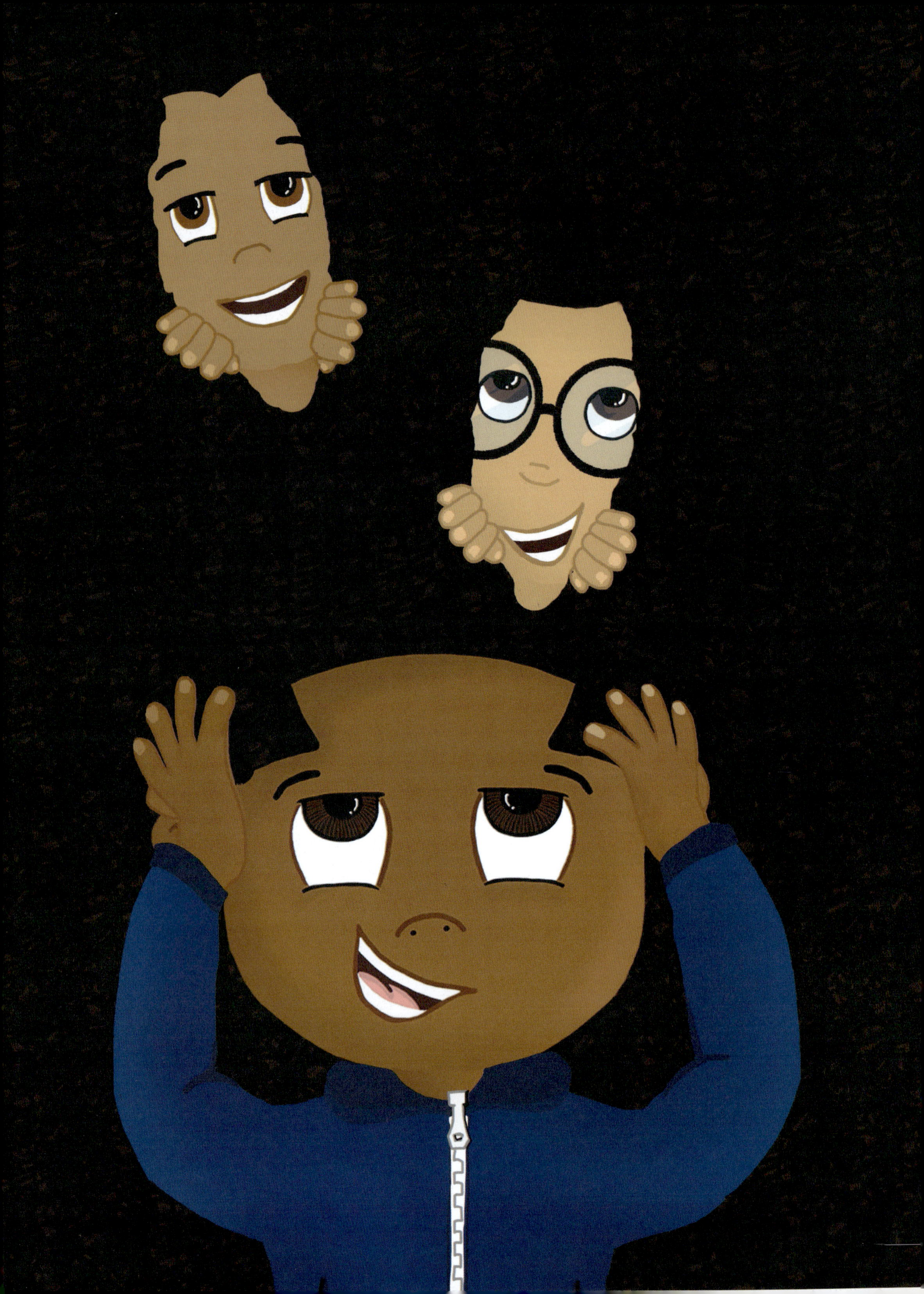

Taye's *hair* grew into a
massive fro it was perfect
for **hide** and seek;
because once *inside*, you could
hide and never be found or seen!

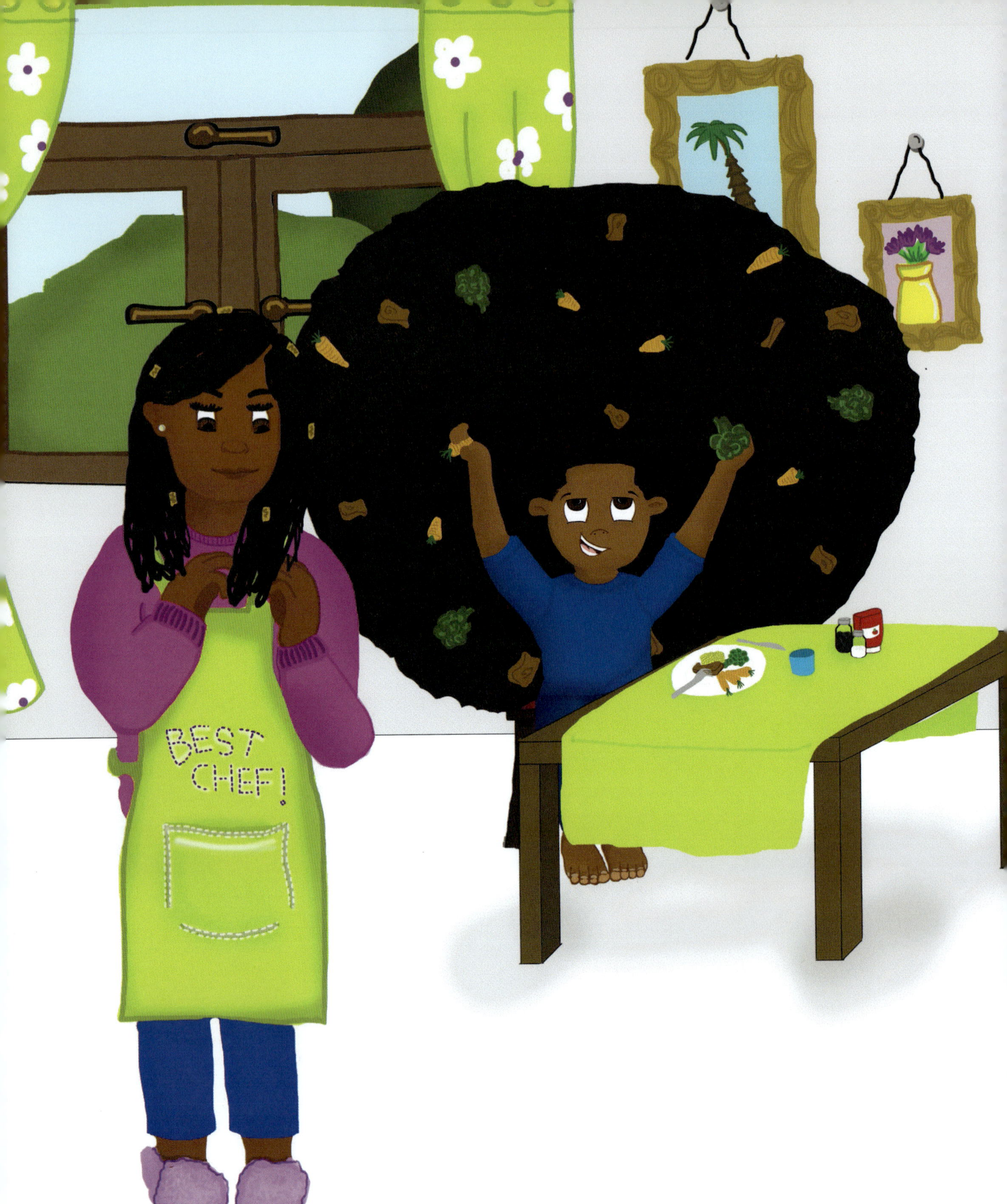
BEST CHEF!

He could **hide** the food he hated
deep *inside* his **fro.**
His mum would think
he **ate** it
but *shhh*
'she doesn't know!'

Taye's *hair* could help him with basketball

boing boing boing

and even with **breakdancing**.

Wohoooo

Wohoooo

AAAHHHHH

Football, his *hair* stopped **all** the players no one could score anything!

But, **KARATE** was his *best* sport, his *hair* made a hand from his **fro**

HI**YAH**

HI**YAH**

Taye's *hair* was **so** *magical* it could help him do them **all!**

Taye's *hair* continued to grow and grow then something **crazy** and **WEIRD** took place. You couldn't guess it even if you tried,

So turn to the next page...

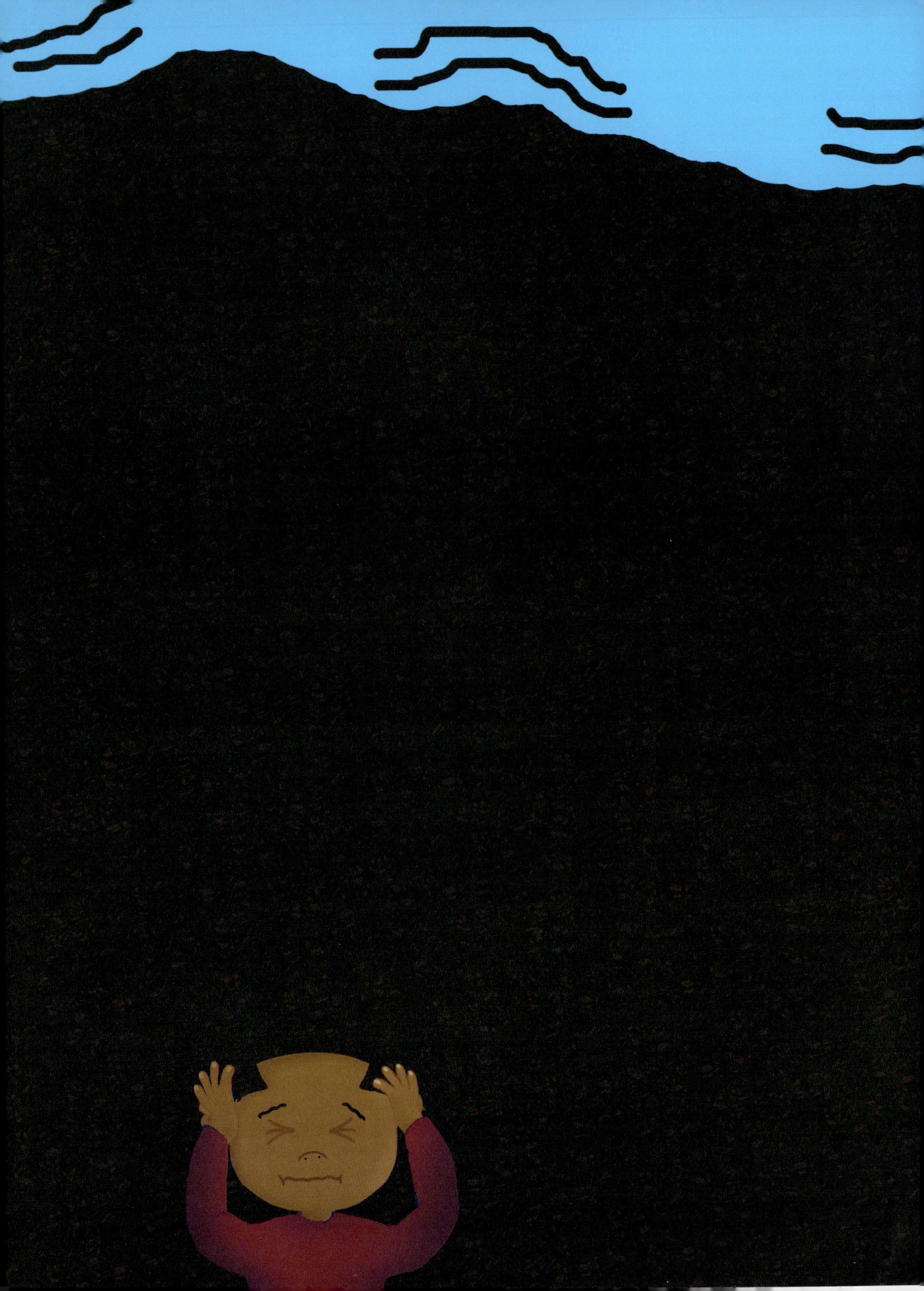

Taye's *hair* so **thick** and coiled it started to...

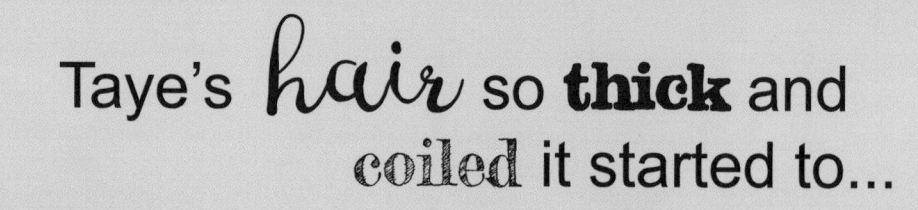

shake...

quiver...

and...

and...

and...

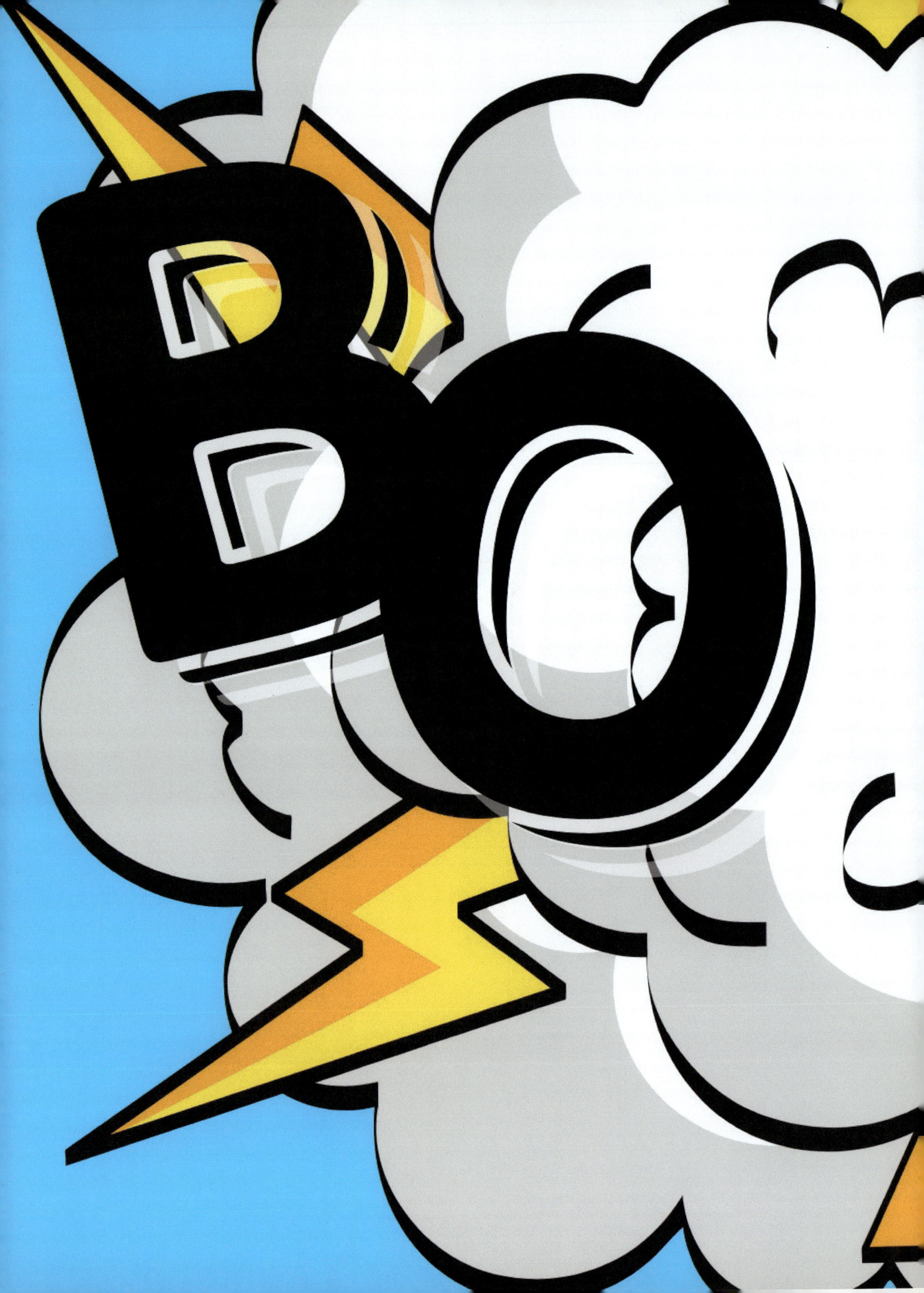
BO

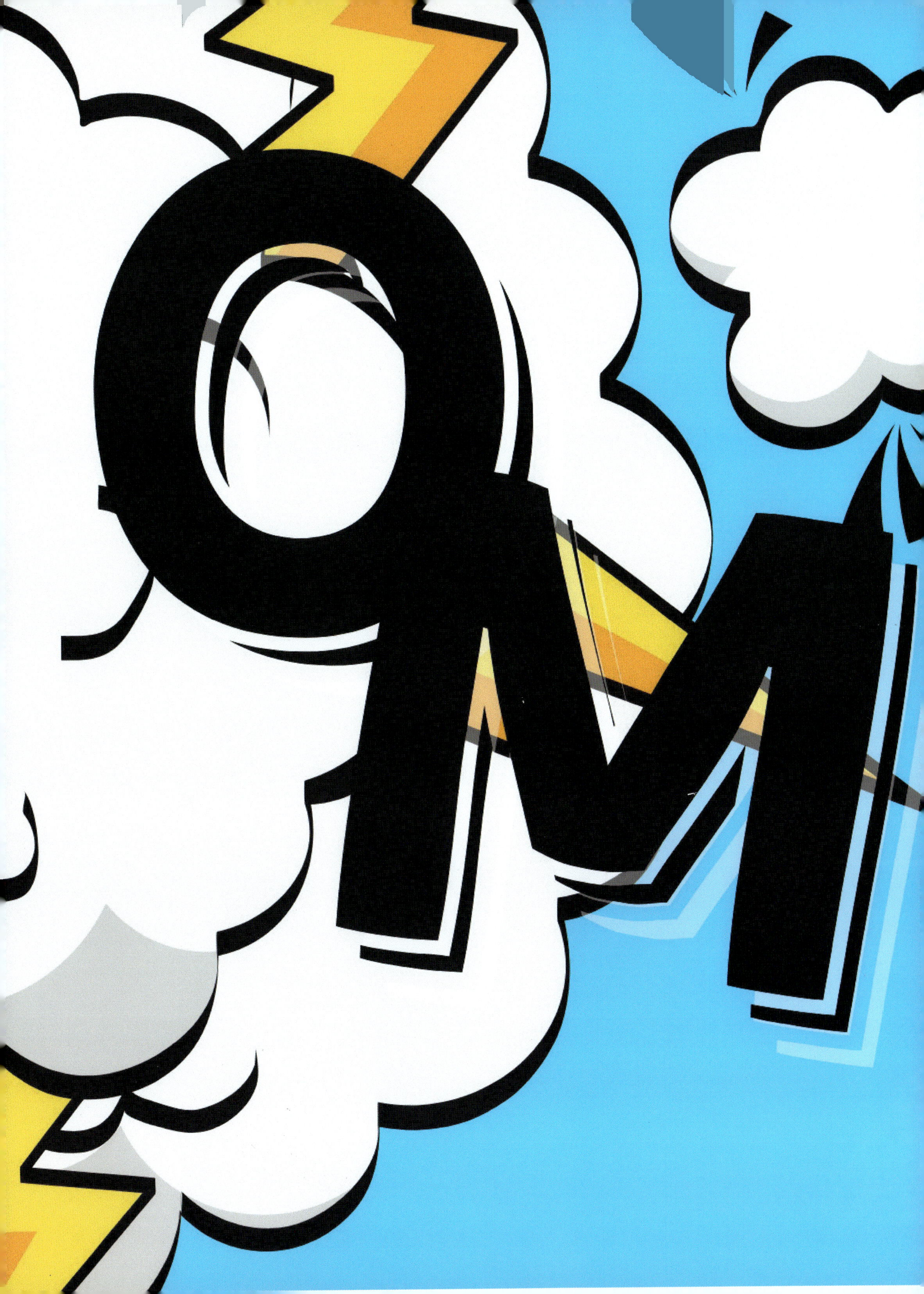
OM

Taye's *hair* turned into a *cosmic - fantastic hair* TIME capsule that started to WHIZZ and ZOOM...

Taye and his best friends -
Jasper, Billy and Sef too;
Jumped onboard the
hair TIME capsule,
There's so much to see and do!"

First, they saw a caveman. **ooga, ooga, ooga** he had a really *hairy* nose and *hair* between his toes...

Off towards the ice age a **Posh** Polar Bear awaits, sipping on his **ICE TEA** isn't that *strange*.

Next on to dinosaur lands roar, rah, roarrrr but, this dinosaur a part from his **roar** was **very strange** and **peculiar**, because he was an **Elvis** fan and liked to eat cans of *tuna*!

This was **REALLY CRAZY**, what was going on, **nothing** seemed to be normal but it was **REALLY fun**...

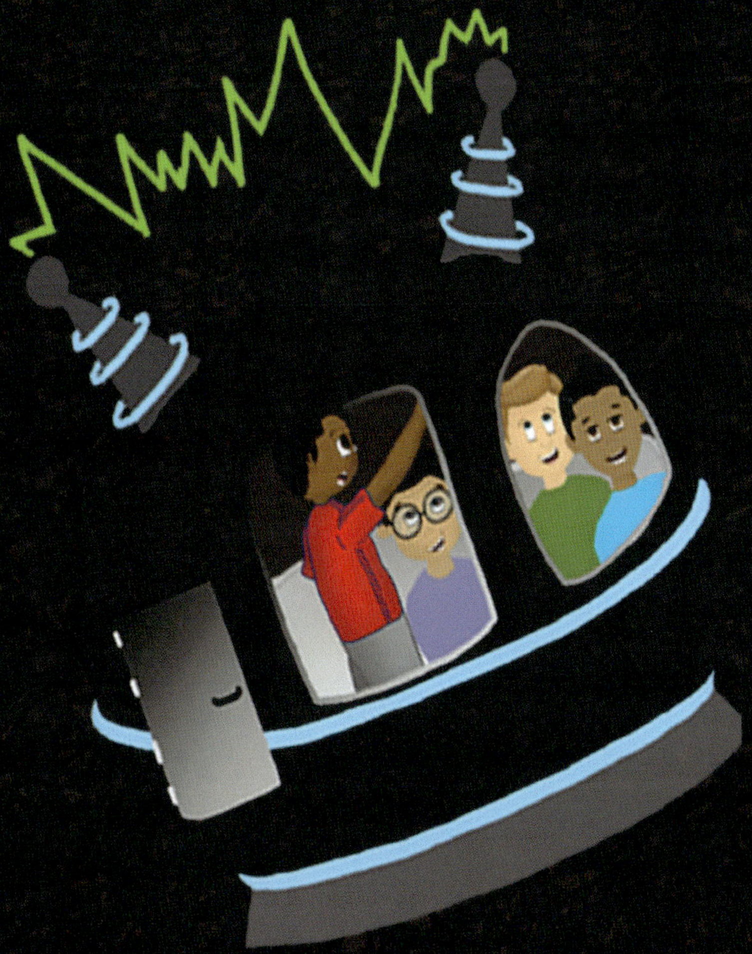

They took the *first steps* on the moon.

Helped to build **upside down** pyramids...

They planted *lots* of seeds and grew the **rainforest.**

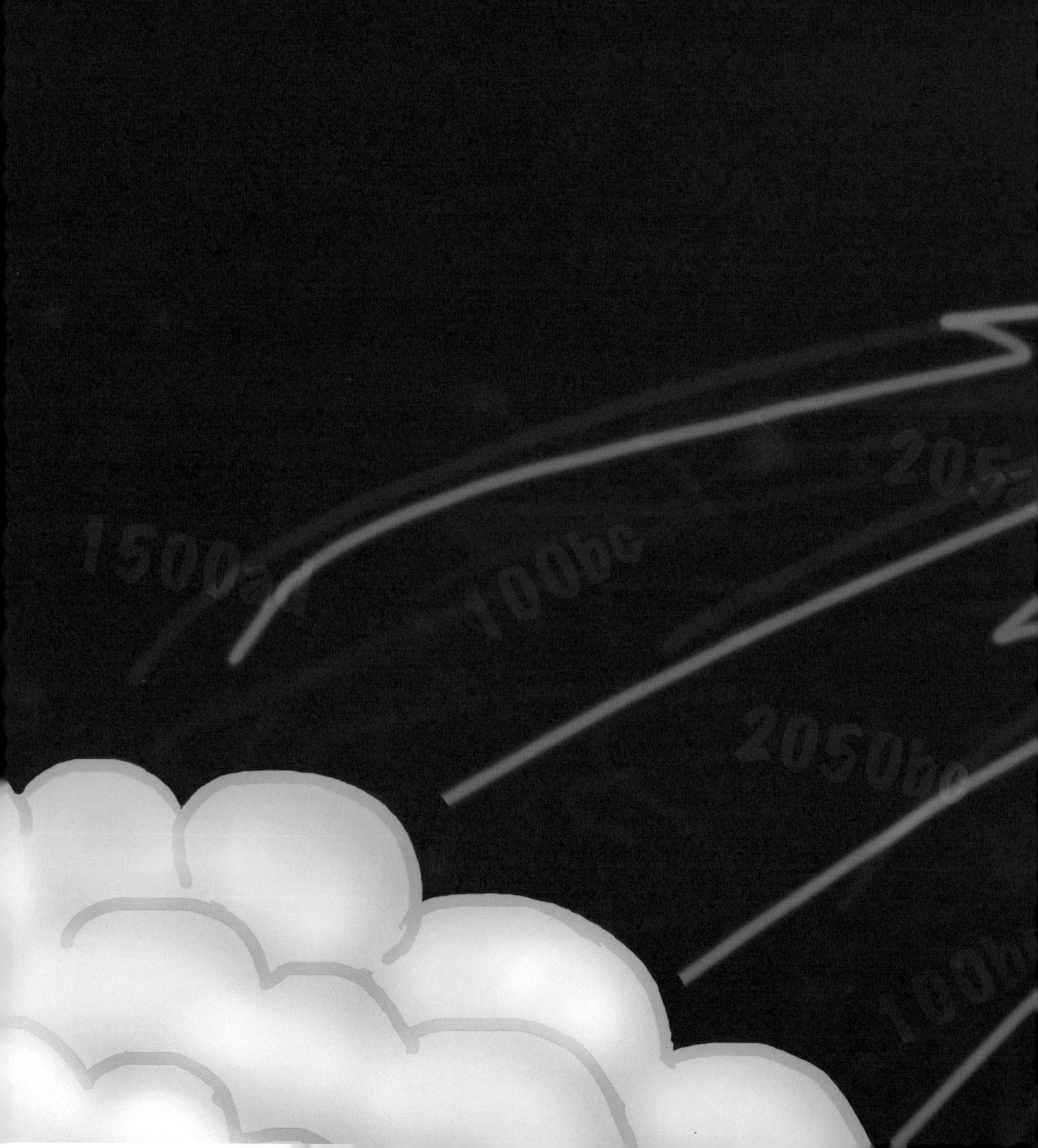

They flew over a million miles
and went **far, far back in time**

Taye's **fro** was something *special*, *no one would understand!*

But all of a sudden
something **strange**
started to happen.

Shake...
quiver...
and...
and...
and...

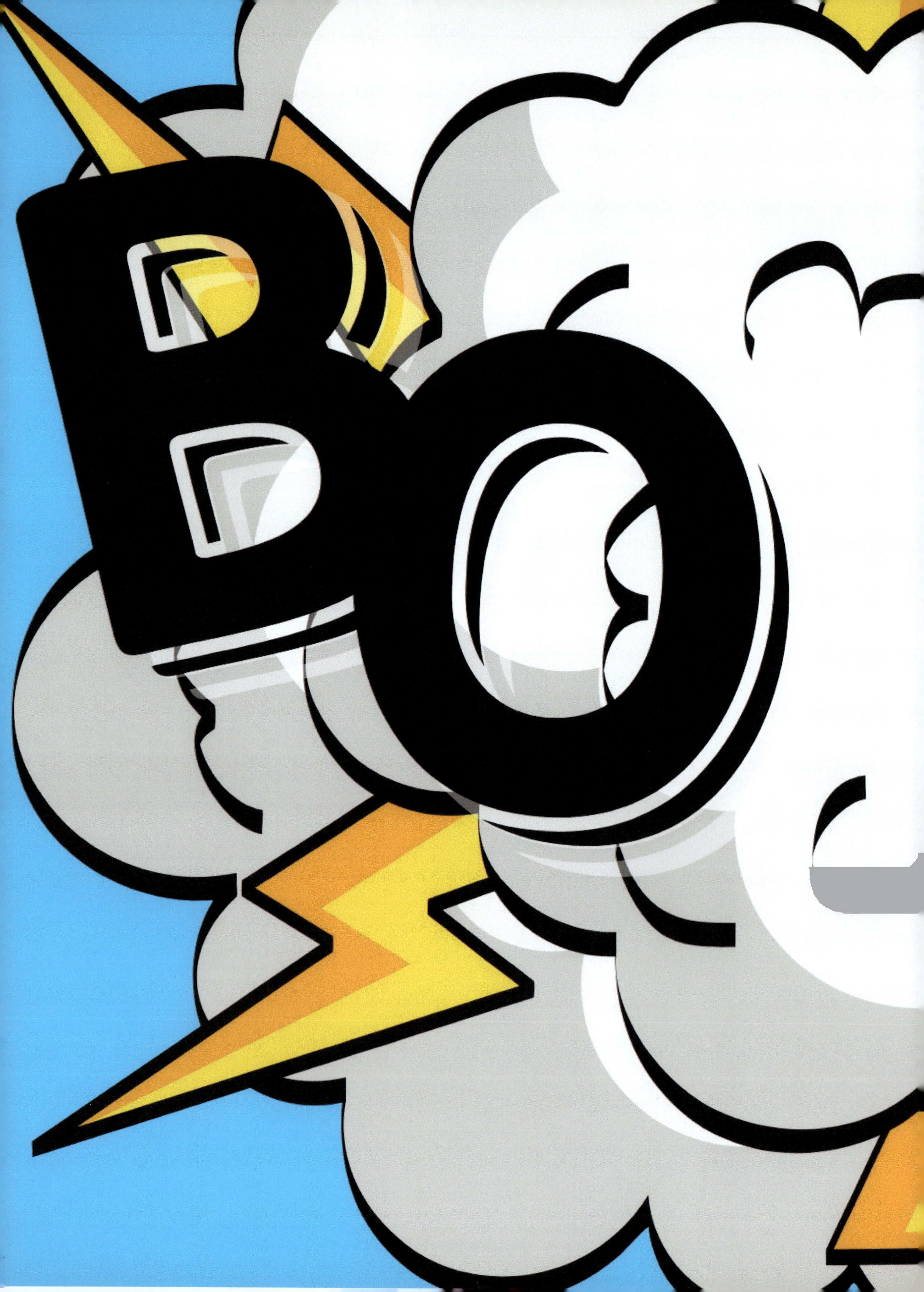
BO

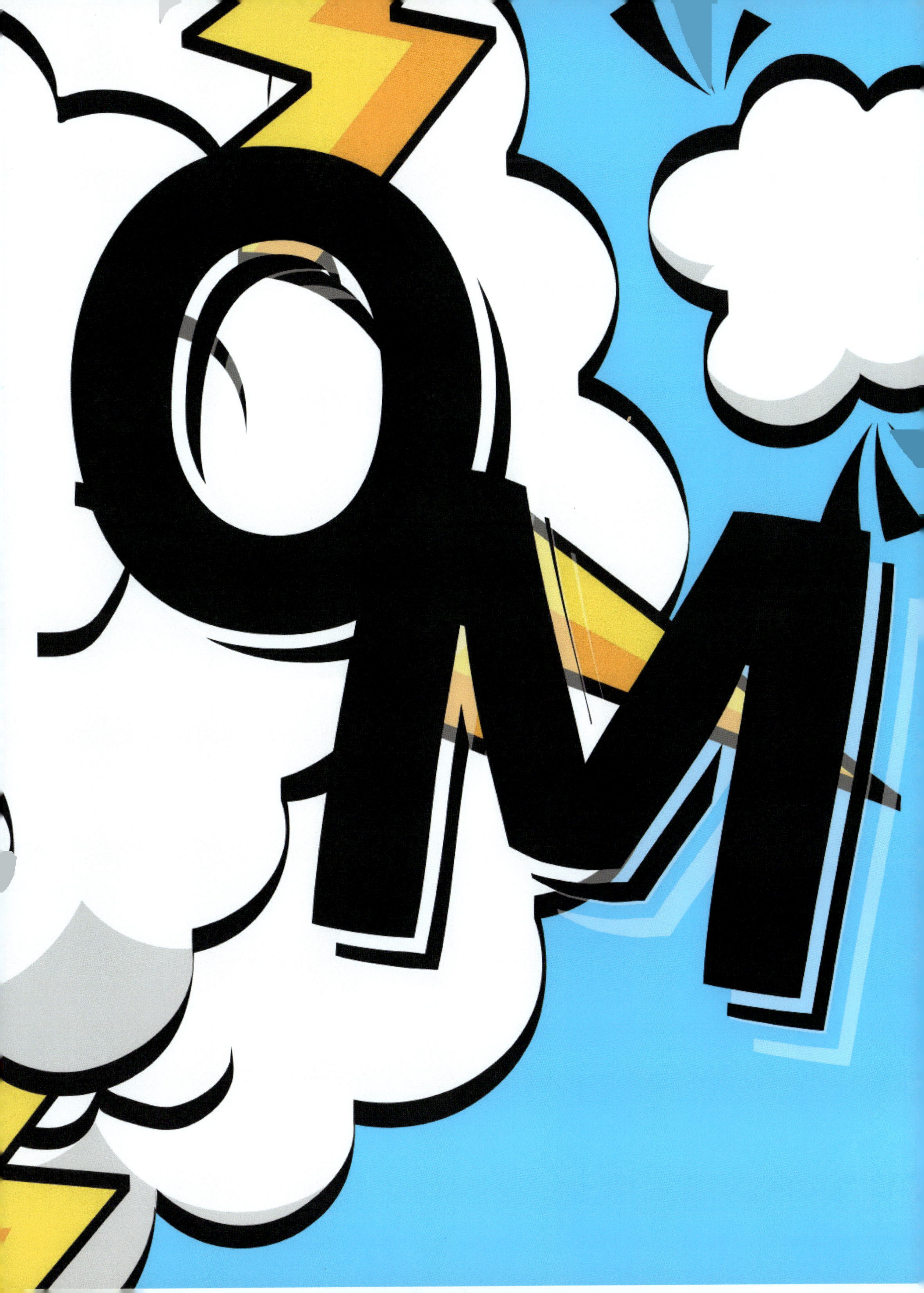
OM

And just like that Taye jumps out of his sleep, wondering what was going on.

Taye feels his hair for his **huge fro**, but, it's no longer super **long!**

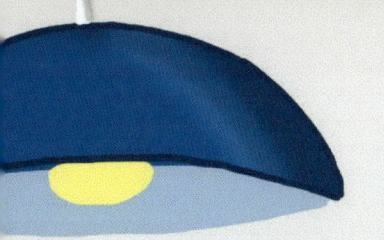

"All of the *hairy* adventure must have been a dream, no wonder it was crazy, I saw things i've never seen!"

And just like that Taye rubbed his eyes and **falls back fast asleep**; Snoring **loudly,** whilst counting sheep... *Was it really a dream?*

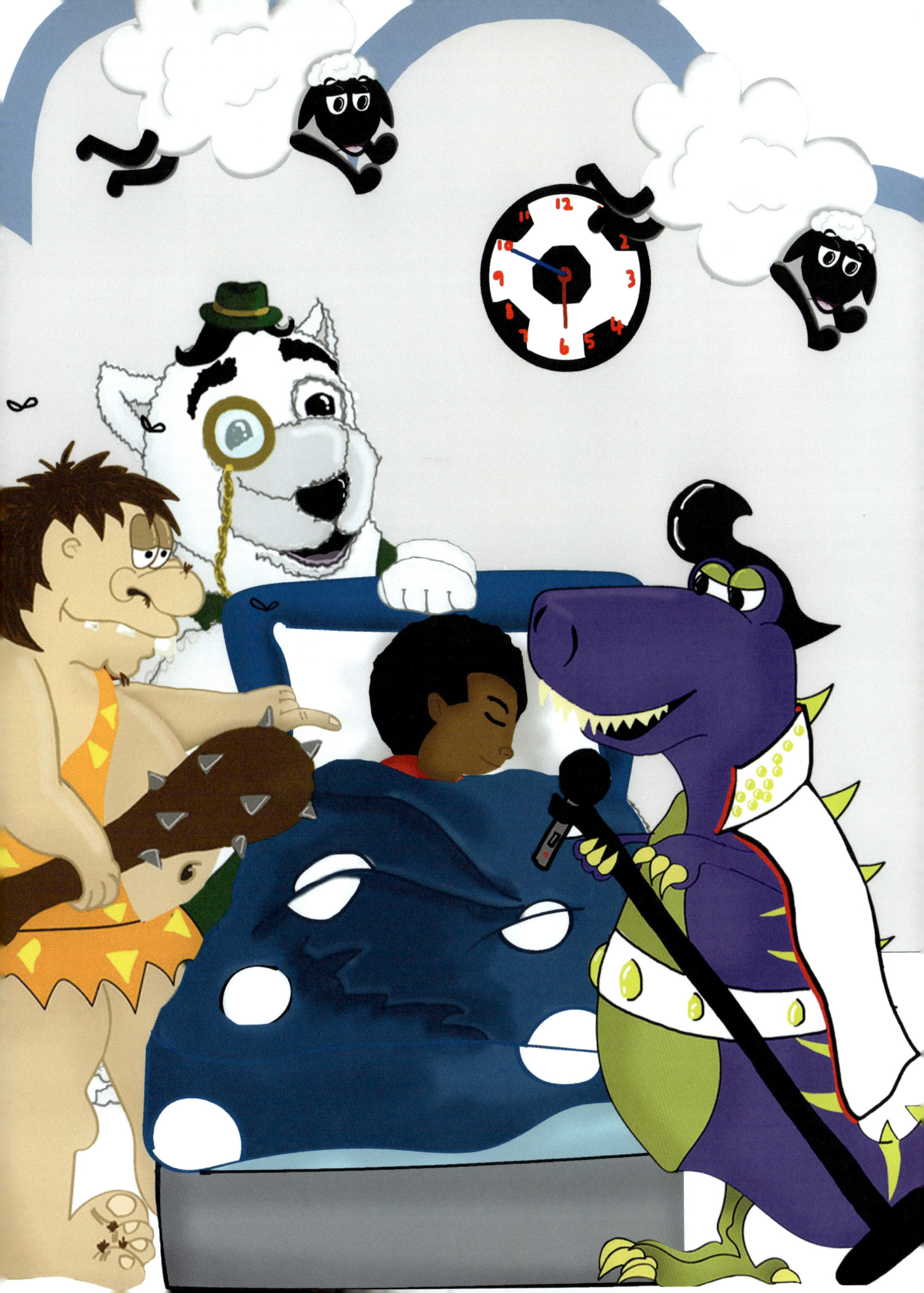

Printed in Great Britain
by Amazon